ACCLAIM FOR THE AUTHOR

"Shauna has touched my life and so many others' lives, both personally and professionally, with her natural ability to get to the core of a person. She truly cares about individual goals and aspirations and helps bring these to light – encouraging people to be their very best. Words cannot describe this woman and what she means to me on so many levels. She is truly a ray of sunshine in times that are not always so bright."

–Abdul H. Rutherford, *Business Specialist*

"It is not often you meet a person who embodies what they teach. Shauna is one of these rare individuals. She has an uncanny ability to simplify complicated systems and interactions, and conveys them in ways that are both digestible and memorable. Her use of humor and seamless incorporation of real-world experience make Shauna (and her work) stand apart from the rest. I am very grateful to have had the pleasure of working with, and learning from Shauna, and am thrilled that so many others will have this opportunity as well."

– Andrew McDonald, *Personal Banker*

Self-published by Shauna Williams
Copyright © 2012 by Shauna Williams

ISBN 978-1-468-11614-4

SECRETS OF A CORPORATE RECRUITER

HOW TO STAND OUT AND GET HIRED.

Shauna Williams

CONTENTS

* * * * * * *

Prologue

Section 1: Q&A

PROLOGUE

These are the day-to-day musings of a corporate recruiter. I hope that some of it will make you laugh. Some of it might shock you. And in some parts of this book, you may even recognize yourself.

I have always believed that finding a J-O-B is more than just creating a resume or filling out an application. You must take a holistic approach to finding that next step in your career. It might take awhile to get to your ultimate dream job, but starting out with the right mind-set is the first step.

Remember this: *We are not defined solely by the position we hold, but by the workings of our inner self; what makes us tick, what makes us happy and gives us energy, rather than taking it away.*

Your J-O-B is what you do. It is not who you ARE.

After reading hundreds of resumes each week, talking to applicants (both over the phone and in person for over 13 years), and recruiting for as many as 400 positions at any time, I know a little bit about what I am doing. Am I the end-all be-all of recruiting? Well, maybe. Why? Because it is important to me and I have paid attention – A LOT of attention over the years – to what makes someone successful and what does not.

I cannot tell you how many times I sit in front of my computer screen talking to faceless applicants: "Really? Are you serious?!"

Everything I really want to say is in the pages of this book. My aim was to create a simple and effective guide to achieving, maintaining and succeeding in your employment search.

I have organized this information into sections based on what I am typically asked during presentations. This should make it easy for you to quickly thumb through to find the information you need, when you need it. If you are not able to find the answer here, please feel free to email me at: shaunawilliams27@yahoo.com

Enjoy. Remember, this is about YOU standing out in a GOOD way and getting noticed. These are the secrets of a corporate recruiter.

Best of luck to you!

SECTION 1: Q&A

* * * * * * *

"I've lost my job. NOW WHAT?!"

This is probably one of the scariest statements made today, in ANY economy. Most of us do not have a back-up plan. Some of us will calmly walk away after being let go (or laid off) and decide to celebrate. "Woo Hoo!! I'm SO glad that I don't ever have to come back to this place!" We may go out and have a drink . . . or even go shopping! Most of us however, will handle the news with a sense of shock and dread.

"How do I tell my family? What do I do next? What bills are due? What can I cut to save money? How much money do I have in savings?" The questions go on and on.

As for me, I went home and went to sleep. (Yes, I too, have been terminated.)

A lot of people panic and rush to "get a job" – the first job they can find. But before you do that, STOP. Take a deep breath, sit quietly and do a self-inventory.

Then sit with someone who knows all about you and loves you anyway. Find that one person you know who will be HELPFUL and not destructive to your spirit. What I mean by that is, sometimes there are people in our lives who can be toxic. They do not mean to be. They probably do not even know they are doing it, but you end up leaving them with a feeling of dread – *gloom and doom*. These are NOT the people I want you to discuss your future with right now.

Think long and hard about the job you just left. What duties did you enjoy *most* and why? Which did you enjoy *least* and why? Was there an unspoken part of that job you cannot quite put a finger on that was so great, or was it mainly that it provided a paycheck?

Now, think about your past jobs. Is there one that stands out as the best job you ever had? Are there jobs you would never do again, no matter what? Ask your friend to remind you of that time in your life. Do they remember you being fulfilled or proud in that past job?

Think about your employment GOALS. Do you just want something to do, or do you want a meaningful career? Perhaps there is a lack of confidence on your part that holds you back from moving forward into the unknown; or is it just a lack of knowledge about the opportunities out there and how to obtain them?

Find out what motivates you and keeps your attention. What would you do whether you were being paid for it or not? What excites you?

I have been singing on stage since the age of nine. I love it. I would do it for free (and I have) because it brings me such satisfaction.

Go back to your childhood. What interested you back then? As children we are free to explore possibilities in ways that, as adults, we have forgotten.

When you are relaxed and at peace, what do you find yourself doing? Are you watching TV shows about cooking? Checking on the stock market? Reading books on self-improvement?

Think of the happiest times in your life. Why were you so happy, and what were you doing at the time? Maybe you were sitting at a desk drawing, or tinkering in the garage, or solving a word puzzle. This may seem strange, especially if it had nothing to do with a job, but I want you to get that feeling in your spirit so that you can begin to recognize what interests you and makes you happy.

Now sometimes it is hard to think about or remember anything positive – especially when you have just lost your job. If that is the case with you, and you are physically able, you can start by getting up out of that chair, couch or bed! I mean literally STAND UP and do something physical. Take a walk. Go for a run. Stand in place and do some jumping jacks. Take your dirty dishes to the sink and turn your vacuum cleaner on – anything to get that blood pumping! Sing at the top of your lungs! Go eat some chili peppers . . . or better yet, CHOCOLATE!

"ARE YOU CRAZY?!"

Well, my friends and family may tell you, "YES!" But there is a method to my madness. You may literally need to stimulate yourself out of your rut. So, GET MOVING!!

We have these wonderful little friends in our brains known as endorphins. *Endorphin* is a combination of two words: *endogenous morphine*, which means "morphine that is created in your brain." Endorphins are activated naturally whenever you do cardio exercise! These little guys are a great way to put the power of optimism back in our lives – if even for a short time – but hopefully long enough for you to do some good self-evaluation!

Once that process is started, take out a notebook and start writing about the things you are now discovering about yourself. Maybe it is just one word that clicks for you, like *people* or *numbers*. Keep going. What is it about *people* that you enjoy? Is it that you need to be around other people to enjoy your job? What does that look like for you? Are you helping them, teaching them or just working alongside them?

Maybe you like *numbers* because you enjoy researching and figuring things out in a more systematic way.

Perhaps you are more comfortable in a creative atmosphere and enjoy taking something from conception (an idea) to fruition (the actual product).

Whatever it is, I cannot help you with that part. This is up to you to figure out. Talk to those non-toxic friends and family. What strengths do they see in you? Listen to them. Take it all in, and along with your own self-assessment, come up with some ideas about your next career move based on your strengths, abilities, skills and preferences.

S E C T I O N 1: Q&A

* * * * * * *

"I've been out of work for 'X' amount of time.
How do I get started again?"
(Stay-at-home moms too.)

This is a tough situation all the way around. In today's economy, it is becoming more and more common. With unemployment rates where they are, many have been unemployed for more than a year – some even longer.

What if you are a woman who decided to stay home and raise your children? That is an honorable thing to do. Many of us moms wish we could have done that too. Just remember, there are a lot of women in the HR profession, including recruiting, so many of us will understand the "stay-at-home mom" thing.

I guess the best approach, overall, is honesty – honesty with yourself and those prospective employers. Take an HONEST look at your past employment and think like a recruiter or hiring manager:

What are the requirements of the job?
    Do you have those skills?
        What have you done to keep those skills up-to-date?

Your experience can be outside the home, inside the home, volunteer work (community, church, sports teams) or otherwise. Be creative. Don't say, "I've JUST been a stay-at-home mom for the past 10 years." You're down-grading yourself. Organizing, prioritizing, multi-tasking, management of time and money – these are all skills that can be transferred to the job market!

But do not be unrealistic either. Chances are you will have to take that entry-level job to get your foot in the door again and work your way up.

Look into classes you can take to increase your knowledge. Maybe you need to brush up on your computer or software skills. How long has it been since you have used MS Excel for instance? Maybe you were a bookkeeper but it has been several years since you have used Quickbooks. Take a refresher course on it.

Other things to consider: Are you *ready* to go back to work full-time? Are there limitations on when you can work (days and hours of the week)? What if the shift requires that you work weekends or evenings? Think about all of these things BEFORE you apply so you can be prepared to answer these "unspoken" questions from the recruiter or hiring manager.

From our perspective, we would much rather know these things up front. Let's say you applied for a position, got a call and came in for an interview. Somewhere during that process you are made aware that you will have to work every other Saturday. You know you either cannot do that or are not willing to. Instead, you say nothing.

Now when they offer you the job and are going over your schedule, you decide to tell them you are unavailable to work Saturdays. Guess what, you have just blown it. They are totally frustrated and ticked off and want to know why you failed to tell them this in the first place.

What's more, you do not get the job and have wasted their time. Do you honestly think they will consider you for any other job in that company? You have also wasted your own time that could have been spent interviewing for another, better-suited-to-you-job. Think about it.

Do not get so caught up in I-just-need-a-job thinking that you stop *thinking* ahead! We have all heard the term "beggars can't be choosers." Do that evaluation BEFORE you continue the interviewing process. Know what your limitations are and what you are willing to do to keep that job once it is offered to you. Please.

But know this: *It is illegal for anyone interviewing you to ask questions about your family; the number of children you have, daycare issues, how you will get to the job* and similar personal questions. If they ask, you might not want to work there because they are either uninformed or knowingly pushing the limits of the laws that protect your privacy.

How do you respond if someone asks a question of this nature? You might try, "I'm not sure how that is relevant to the job." That should shut them up. If it does not, then seriously re-think working there. It could be an indication that they will not follow the rules in other areas too.

Sometimes, when an interview is going well you might be tempted to relax a little and start talking about your kids or family. Face it, if you have been a stay-at-home mom, your children have been your life and everything you think about surrounds them. A prospective employer may not have the same perspective, so be cautious about what you say. This goes for other personal information as well.

A hiring manager wants to know what you will bring to the table for their company. Period. So, even in casual conversation, just make a mental note to yourself not to talk about it. Focus on you and your abilities.

In the end, what it takes is preparation and honesty, but not full disclosure.

SECTION 1: Q&A

* * * * * * *

"I want to change careers after 'X' amount of years. What do I do now?"

This is also a tough one. It is important to show stability and continuity on your resume, but what happens if the field you are in suddenly dries up – like the IT boom in the late 1990s or the mortgage market in 2008? A career change may just be inevitable. What do you do then?

Take a deep breath.

Think about the skills you have developed in those jobs. How would they transfer into a new career? Do some research on careers that are of interest to you. If at all possible, talk to someone experienced in the field. Ask them what their day looks like. What are their job duties and responsibilities? Would they choose that career again if they had the chance? If not, why? What are the pros and cons to this type of work? Remember, do your RESEARCH first.

If you have decided on a new career, learn about the job requirements. Is a degree typically required? Where does your current schooling place you on that list? What type of experience are they usually looking for and do you have it? If not, are there entry-level positions you could do to learn along the way? What do they typically pay?

Can you AFFORD to make that change? What if your household is used to an income of $50K a year, but this new career starts out at only $25K? How would you make that adjustment? How will you answer that question when the recruiter says something like this: "I see you were making over $50K a year. What are your salary expectations for this job?" Because we WILL ask. And if we do not, that could be a bad sign and you will need to answer it *for* us. So be prepared.

Get out and talk to people. Network! Find out if there are associations you can join – Chambers of Commerce – where someone from that field is represented. Do you have friends, family members or associates who might know someone who knows someone? Ask if you can do an *informational interview* with someone in your new field of interest.

Check out facebook, LinkedIn and other social media sites to see if you can find contacts there, then MAKE CONTACT.

This is a challenge, for sure, but well worth it if it puts you on a path that fulfills not only your financial needs but gives you that passion you are looking for in a career and fills you with excitement.

SECTION 1: Q&A

* * * * * * *

"How do I get past the 'I was fired' stigma?"

My belief is always (again) – HONESTY – above all else. If you made a mistake and were fired, be honest about it. If you did not make a mistake and were fired, be honest. If you do not know WHY you were fired . . . you guessed it, be honest.

Now, hear me on this: *You do NOT need to fill the recruiter's ears with a sob story, boss-bashing or catty talk about a former co-worker.*

K.I.S.S. – Keep it Simple Sweetie. Take it from me, we DO NOT want all the gory details, and we definitely do not want to hear you talk about what a jerk your former boss was! What if we know that person? We are in the industry. There is a chance we just might. What if we call for work references and get that same manager on the line? Please be careful and avoid the negativity. Try to put a positive spin on it . . . but be honest!

Look at it from the recruiter's standpoint. What did you LEARN from that experience? If you were let go due to too many attendance issues, what have you done to overcome those issues now?

A colleague and I were interviewing a young man who admitted that he had been fired from his last two jobs. I asked him what the terms of the departure were and he said that it was because of tardiness and missing work. My colleague and I glanced at each other with "the look" that said, "Okay. Let's cut this one short!"

But here is what happened: This young man went on to tell us that he now realized it was a problem and one that he had not fully dealt with up to that point. He knew that if he did not figure out a way to correct the problem, he was going to continue having difficulty finding a job, as he had been on several previous interviews (he admitted to us), and had not been hired. He recognized what we in the hiring industry already know: *Your past behavior can be an indicator of your future performance.*

What he told us next made us stop our "let's hurry this one up" process and actually listen to him. What he had been doing wrong was setting his cell phone alarm and keeping it next to his bed. When the alarm went off, he would immediately turn it off. (Many of us wake up like this). The problem is that some of us go right back to sleep. (I know, I did it this morning.) This was his problem also.

So he solved it by buying an old-fashioned alarm clock that was very loud and would not turn off automatically. He placed it clear across the room from where he slept. When it went off five minutes later, he had to get up out of bed to turn it off . . . and *voila!!* He was awake and had resolved his issues of going back to sleep.

And do you know what? This inspired my co-interviewer and myself to continue the interview. The young man showed us that he was willing to make that extra effort to change his bad habit and we had a pretty good idea that he would likely not make that same mistake again.

He was hired.

SECTION 1: Q&A

* * * * * * *

"I'm a 'mature' worker who wants to work, but no one seems interested. Help!"

I say, "Viva La Old Fart!" Let's face it, more and more of us Baby Boomers (did I just admit how old I am?), are continuing to work well into our 60s and 70s. We have a vast wealth of experience and, typically, a great work ethic. We are valuable! Now, how do you get a young, Gen-Y'er to see that? (Gen-Y is the generation of people born during the 80s and early 90s).

Personality. Vibrance. Energy. A big ol' fat smile on your face! Don't show them your chronological age, but your *agelessness*.

How do we apply this to finding a job? Resumes should NOT reflect every single job you have ever had over the past 40 years! You need to be a little creative here. Take a close look at the job description. Do you have that experience? Was it 20+ years ago? Okay. Put it on your resume (and this is probably the only time I am going to tell you not to put dates), but under the title "Additional Experience" or "Related Experience."

You still want to list what you have been doing the past 5-10 years, but if it is different than the job you are interested in, just put a minimal explanation of your duties.

Let's say you owned an insurance agency for the past 25 years. You made a lot of money, managed several staff, created and maintained a healthy customer base. Now, you are retired but you do not want to completely stop working. You think it would be fun to work in a bank as a teller.

In 1982, before starting your insurance company, you worked in a bank (which is now defunct), as a teller. You loved that job because you got to see people all the time, work with money and stay busy. You would like to work part-time hours and the branch is just down the street from your house. Sounds perfect, right?

Here is what you do. First, DO YOUR RESEARCH. Do the hours offered in the job posting match what you are looking for? Do you know what the branch hours are? Have you read up on this bank (when it was established, where it ranks in size and status, what it is 'known' for, etc.)?

Now go into that branch on a Tuesday or Wednesday. (Mondays and Fridays are the busiest days of the week in a branch, or anywhere, really.) Ask to speak with the manager. Remember, you have an advantage because you do not look like a kid looking for a job. You look like a potential customer.

When the manager greets you, ask for just a few minutes of his or her time. SMILE. Be open and friendly. Explain that you are very interested in working there and why, and that you are willing to work the hard-to-fill hours (evenings, weekends or lunch coverage).

Tell the manager that you have already gone *on-line and completed your application* and you just wanted to come in and introduce yourself and offer a paper copy of your resume. Thank the manager for his or her time and be prepared to leave.

If the manager is interested, he or she will let you know. They may even sit you down right then and there for an informal interview. Be prepared! Have a few copies of your resume handy. Be willing and flexible. Do not have a "tee time" to get to while you just "run in" to talk to the manager. Keep an open schedule and be ready to talk about yourself to this person – who could very well offer you a job on the spot – IF you are prepared.

S E C T I O N 1: Q&A

* * * * * * *

"I don't see a lot of people who look like me in this company. Should I even try to get a job here?"

Ah . . . my soapbox. Not only am I of mixed race, but so are my children. I also used to weigh 300 pounds and my best friend in the world was gay! Depending on the part of the country where you live, the subject of *diversity and inclusion* may or may not be an issue for you. However, I have found that for many this is a key issue.

The face of America is changing. According to the United States Census Bureau, 27% of its population in 2010 were non-White or people of color. However, by 2050 it is estimated the percentage of minorities will increase to 54%. The U.S. Census Bureau defines "minorities" as everyone except for non-Hispanic, single race Whites. (Information source: *America 2050: Minorities in Majority*, CNN.com, August 13, 2008)

If you can relate to the above statement, my suggestion is this: Research the company you are interested in working for. Go to the company website and see if they list *diversity and inclusion* as an integral part of their company. Do they have a diversity initiative that is clearly listed and easily accessible? Notice details like the pictures of people on their web page. Are they diverse?

If you are able, visit this company. Who greets you? Who do you see walking around, sitting at desks, behind the counter? Do you see people who look like you? Perhaps this is an indication of a "behind-the-scenes" attitude or belief system this company has in regard to diversity and inclusion.

Does the company have formal *affinity groups* or a *diversity council*? Visit diversity.com and see if the company is listed and what, if anything, is noted about it. Start or find a blog; ask questions of your friends, family and associates. What have they heard about this company? Check LinkedIn, facebook and twitter.

Aside from all of that – and depending on how you feel – ask yourself this question: "Do I want to work for this company after all the information I have found (or not found)?" If the answer is "yes" then go for it!

I have presented countless job-ready workshops with communities of color, disadvantaged youth, mature workers, prison inmates, the differently-abled and other diverse groups. The unspoken truth is that if you do not ask the question, these groups will not tell you. *Diversity and support in the workplace is essential to success, not only for the organization, but for the people who work there.*

So what do you do if you fit into one of these wonderfully unique and diverse groups and you *still need a job*? I may be fishing in delicate waters here, but I am going to put myself out there and do something a lot of HR people will not do. I am going to tell the truth.

Does racism, sexism, homophobia and ageism exist in America? Oh, heck ya! The truth of the matter is that employers DO see color, sexual orientation, weight and physical appearance – EVEN THOUGH WE ARE NOT SUPPOSED TO. And NO ONE would EVER admit that! We notice the name on the top of the resume and voice patterns and inflections when we talk to you on the phone.

As I have said before: *Take a long, hard look at yourself. What are your goals? Where is your passion when it comes to a career? How much of a priority is it for you to seek and find that career?*

You may find conflict between your goals and the reality of most dominant culture-run businesses. Make sure that you BALANCE these goals and principals with what YOU are willing to do. This is important because many, many times, people in positions of power at these companies DO NOT REALIZE they are being discriminatory.

You may have to consider dressing like them and talking like them and playing the game. And if you do, then beat them at their own game.

The Art of War by Sun Tzu says: "Victorious warriors win first and then go to war, while defeated warriors go to war first and then seek to win."

Plan, Prepare, Perform and Persevere in order to win your success!

If you will not compromise who you are to fit the mold, then I say this, "I hear you. I feel you. I respect you and I AGREE with you." But depending on the job you want, you just might have to anyway. That is the sad reality.

It should not be a Me vs. You, or an Us vs. Them thing. It takes a strong individual to think it through and make a commitment to bettering his or her life. But isn't that the same for everyone's success? This is about a means to an end. It is not just your J-O-B that makes you happy in life but who you are as a person; your family, friends and outside accomplishments that fulfill your life. I am not recommending that you sell yourself short for anything or anyone! Just KNOW YOURSELF and what you are willing to do.

Set yourself a goal to BECOME the hiring manager at your company and make that change yourself. BE the change you want to see!

My experience has been that many White people do not believe racism still exists. I once relayed a painful story to a co-worker (who is White) about my previous partner (who is Black) driving down a particular street near us, then being followed and pulled over by a police officer for no other apparent reason than *racial profiling* – simply because he is Black.

My co-worker responded, "Well, I'VE never noticed racism there before."

I politely reminded him that he would not necessarily have noticed it because he is White and it had never happened to him before.

It is easy enough to say, "Walk a mile in my shoes," but we cannot really begin to understand what another person goes through – their obstacles and struggles – without being that person. I always told my partner that no matter how much I loved him, felt for him and understood his pain, I would NEVER know what it was like to be a Black man.

We, as hiring managers and recruiters need to do a better job of being open to hiring people who do not look like us or share the same interests, culture or traditions. Most hiring managers hire people they have things in common with – chiefly language, culture and religion. Understanding that diversity goes way beyond being a catch-phrase and actually HIRING people and supporting them at the workplace is the *key to success* for any company.

SECTION 1: Q&A

* * * * * * *

"I have my college degree and I'm ready to take over the company! Why won't anyone hire me?"

What I have found in my career is that often when someone is graduating from college they expect to land this "great" job right away. This may happen in some instances, but if you have only put in your time at school and do not have any actual work history, this can be a challenge.

It is not that no one will hire you. A lot of companies put a great deal of emphasis on someone with a degree. However, in today's economy,* when someone applies for a job that requires experience in that field and they do not have it, they may be passed over. The job will go to the person who not only has the educational background, but the hands-on work experience.

How do you balance this? Well, one way is to accept internships and job-shadowing, and attend events where people in your desired field hang out. Consider joining the local chapter of your Chamber of Commerce (there will be a fee), or other affiliate groups. Request an informational interview with someone in your desired position. Ask where he or she started and progressed, and consider modeling your career on his or hers. Get a <u>LinkedIn</u> account and start networking on-line.

If you have not already started this during your college years, then get started now! Hiring managers want to see that you took the initiative and sought out opportunities before you graduated (or as soon after as possible). Think of it as extended study. Many colleges can link you to programs and associations in your field of study.

Networking is also a wonderful way to make those connections. When someone gets to know you and sees your willingness to go above and beyond to further your career, this will impress them. Perhaps someone in one of these organizations owns a company in your field, and because they have gotten to know you, might be willing to give you an opportunity. You will never know if you do not put yourself out there!

A college education is a wonderful, admirable thing.

I do not personally have a degree. I started working directly out of high school at Intel Corporation. I worked my way up rather quickly, but that had more to do with my ambition, ability and personality (sunny disposition and serious work ethic). These are really the characteristics that in the end, hiring managers are looking for.

You can compare two people with similar resumes, education and work experience and try to make a decision based on those concrete facts. But I will tell you that the person who gets the job, nine times out of ten, is the one with the personality, great attitude, communication skills, motivation and, dare I say it, *people skills.*

Definitely work toward higher education! But along the way, I hope you have started to get some work experience that will lend itself to your desired field. If you have not, keep in mind you might have to take that entry-level position as an aquarist before realizing your dream of becoming a Marine Biologist.

At the time of this writing, the national unemployment rate is over 8%.

SECTION 1: Q&A

* * * * * * *

"I'm unhappy in my current job and considering quitting. What should I do?"

DON'T QUIT! I tell people this all the time. What should you do? Start re-thinking your life. What is making you so unhappy in your job? Is it the work itself? Is it the hours or schedule? Is it your manager or co-workers? What? Are things going on at home or in your personal life that are really at the root of your unhappiness?

Once you figure that out, do some research on other occupations that are of interest to you. Or resolve your personal issues. Remember, we are complex human beings made up of life experiences, emotions and personal challenges along WITH our work history. What you do not want to do is react emotionally before thinking things through first. Make that plan, prepare (do your research), perform the activities needed to accomplish your goals and persevere throughout. You might not find success your first time out.

Choose the things that you DO enjoy in your current job and use that experience to get your foot in the door elsewhere.

YOU could be a bank teller:

At a bank, a teller is someone who works face-to-face with the general public. They handle money (counting back change, balancing their cash drawer), use a computer and talk to customers about products and services the bank offers (sales). They also stand all day long. They may have to carry coin bags that weigh up to 50 pounds.

Let's say you have worked at a fast food restaurant for the past year. You realize you are not going to move mountains in that job, so you start looking at other options BEFORE you quit. Even if you are only getting 10 hours a week, that is 10 HOURS of PAY, which is better than no pay at all if you quit without having another job lined up. And believe me, we recruiters look at things like that, because it can speak to a person's *decision-making ability* and sense of *responsibility*.

You could apply to be a teller at a bank. They generally pay better than fast food, it is a cleaner environment and, typically you have much more room to grow your career. And guess what? You would qualify for that position.

Sometimes your job is a means to an end. For many of us, it is our personal activities and functions that keep us inspired and motivated. These are things you can do while still working to provide you with a sense of accomplishment and pride.

Join a community group, get active or write those letters and emails you keep thinking about. Take an art class. Reconnect with your family and friends. Find something that GIVES you energy rather than takes it from you. Think about what inspires you. Sometimes, that is where we find our next job! Maybe that class you decide to take will lead you down another path you had never considered before. Maybe you will meet someone in that class (or group) with interests similar to yours. They may introduce you to others and something will develop from there.

The bottom line is, *it all depends on your attitude*. In the book, <u>Fish!</u> by Steven Lundin, Harry Paul and John Christensen, Mary Jane is a woman who inherits a group to manage at the bank. They are called, the "Toxic Energy Dump" because of their negative attitudes and apathy. People avoid any interaction with this group because of this. Out of the four principals outlined in the book, the fourth principal is the one that applies best here. It is "Choose Your Attitude." If you look for negativity, you will find it. It is a choice! You are not helpless; but you ARE responsible for your actions or in-actions.

I know how it feels to be in a job where you do not feel appreciated, noticed or valued. Maybe there is a co-worker or manager who seems to have it out for you. You feel frustrated, indignant, or just plain old fed up. You want to react or you have allowed them to deflate your purpose.

Always look within first. Is it possible that YOU might be the problem? If you have tried communicating with that person by being honest and owning your own perception of the situation without blaming or pointing fingers and you still have not seen improvement, then make a plan. Map out the steps you need to take to either deal with the person or situation on a daily basis (i.e., just focus on the positive aspects of the job), or find a way to get out of that department or company.

Do not give your personal power away! You have greatness in you. Focus on and hold fast to that.

SECTION 2: DOS & DO NOTS

* * * * * * *

DO NOT use proprietary words on your resume, especially if you are applying outside of your field of work. We recruiters may not know what a hydro-electrical engineer is. Or what an "FA2" is. We may call a particular job title something completely different. Think instead about the skills and duties of those jobs; the certificate, license or degree required. DO have a friend (who is not in the same field), take a look at your resume and see if they can figure out what you did.

•

DO NOT claim something you cannot back up! "Good knowledge of banking," when there is no banking experience on your resume, is one example.

•

DO read the job description! I really want to say, "READ the DA&# job description!" You have no idea how many resumes I open and then scream, "Did you even READ the job description?! Reeeally?" They are a waste of my time. And if I see your name too many more times applying for every job available within the company, I may not take the time to consider you for the job you might actually be qualified for, because you have already shown me you did not do your homework in the first place.

If you DO feel strongly about a position and believe that you fit what the job description and requirements are asking for, then DO the work for the recruiter. Make it obvious why you are applying for this particular job. DO NOT make us do the work for you. We might have active imaginations, but please do not assume that we can read your mind when it comes to applying for a particular job. In short, DO NOT apply for the job if you are not qualified for the position!

Out-of-state applicants: It may be difficult to catch the attention of the recruiter unless the job is a niche position with very specific qualifications. Entry-level positions will generally go to a local candidate.

If you are truly ready to relocate if you get the job, DO find a way to make that evident. Explain it in your cover letter, on your application or at the top of your resume. Why? Because if a recruiter is looking at your address and the position is in the next state or across the country, your resume may have just taken a dumpster dive. Sometimes the hiring manager will tell us that they do not want to look at anyone who is not local.

DO make us understand that you are MOTIVATED to move! Does your wife's family live there? Did you grow up there and want to return to the area? Whatever the reason, do not say, "I'll move there if the offer is right." Guess what? Unless you have the skills and experience that are an exact match for the position, there will probably never be an offer. You DO have to convince us to look at you. Saying something like, "I've always wanted to live in California," is not enough motivation.

•

Assume that if you have done the work, you have the job (confidence counts), but DO NOT stop looking and interviewing until you have the actual offer in hand. A good friend of mine was sure she had gotten her dream job. She gave notice to her current employer and started making plans to move across the country and she had not even received a verbal offer. She was their second choice. Oops.

•

DO make sure your phone works! I understand that sometimes when we have been out of work it is often difficult to pay that phone bill. But keep this in mind, if that is the only way to reach you, DO NOT wonder why you are not getting called. Make it a priority or DO give another (reliable) phone number on your resume or online application.

•

When creating your own voice mail message, DO keep it professional! You do not have to be super dry or "robotic" about it, but I once actually heard, "Love ya!" as a phone message. Christian music played before her voice came on (which is fine if you don't mind that kind of music), but reeeally? You LOVE ME? Come on.

Also, while extremely cute, please DO NOT let your kids create your voice mail message. Remember to keep it professional.

•

When leaving a voice message, DO slow down! Give your name and phone number along with a short message about why you are calling. Enunciate. You might want to plan ahead what you will say and practice it so you do not stutter and stumble over your words at "the sound of the beep."

If English is not your first language, please slow down when speaking and really work on speaking clearly. If you have an uncommon name, remember to spell it.

If you are in a crowded area be aware of that. Sometimes background noise can be so distracting to the person listening to your message that they cannot understand everything you have said. DO NOT try to leave a message when the TV is blaring. Find a time and quiet place to return a call.

•

DO check your spelling and the phone numbers you have written on your application. I was truly interested in speaking with a gentleman about a job, but when he filled out the application, he transposed two digits in his phone number. I kept calling the wrong number (obviously) and it just so happens that the person whose number I was calling did not have a voice message with a specified name. So after leaving two messages and no return call, I was about to give up on the guy. Another recruiter might have stopped trying, but I went the extra step and sent him an email. When he contacted me by the phone number listed on my email address, I asked about his number. It was then we discovered his error.

If I had not taken the extra step to contact him another way, he would have been left wondering why no one had called him. Instead, he got the job!

•

If you have worked at temporary agencies (staffing companies), please do NOT list every job you have had through them unless they were long-term contracts. Instead, talk about the skills required of you. Recruiters understand temp agencies and their purpose. We do not need to know the details on every assignment you were given there. If there were many different assignments and companies, then list the commonality between them. Were you a receptionist at each company? Were you repeatedly asked back by this company because they liked your work? Did you offer a skill set that went beyond what the employer originally needed, and were you hired because of this? Be creative when presenting yourself.

From the business side, companies use temp services because they are not responsible to pay for unemployment insurance, workers compensation insurance or any of the other things a company usually pays for a regular, full time employee. That is the beauty of these services. Companies pay the fee per hour (which includes the temp's pay and the fee to the agency), and they can send that person packing for any reason (within the limits of the law).

Sometimes a person starts out as a temp on a long-term contract (six months or more), and eventually becomes an employee of that company. This is something that you would highlight on your resume, as it speaks volumes to your work ethic and abilities.

If you did leave an assignment, be sure to explain why. It may have only been a two-week assignment and you stayed the entire length of that contract. It was not because you did something wrong or because you did not fulfill the needs of the business. Be sure to explain that too.

I am a big supporter of temp services, not only for a business, but because, as an individual, you can gain experience working for different companies while learning new skills or staying current on the skills you already have.

SECTION 3: RESUME-WRITING

* * * * * * *

I often hear, "I've applied for a hundred different jobs. Why am I not getting any calls back?"

Good question! To answer that, we have to look at the big picture.

It is a matter of perception. I once heard this analogy: Have you ever been to an art gallery and looked up close at an actual oil painting? If you stand two inches away from that painting, what do you see? A bunch of "blobs" of paint, right? Now, take a step back. You see a little more. Another step back and you see the whole painting, which then allows you to understand how that initial "blob" of paint fits into the whole picture.

We may wonder why bad things happen to us. Without knowing or "seeing the big picture" we get confused, angry, sad and sometimes desperate. But when we step back (sometimes years later) we see how that event fit into, or became a part of our life (the blobs). It may not have been pretty by itself or had meaning at the time, but now you can see why it needed to be there to create its place in our big picture.

Think about your life journey to this point. Since we spend so much of our waking time at a job, it really is an integral part of our lives. Remember, our job is not WHO we are, but what we do.

It is important to take a step back and look at our big picture. Are we on the path to our goals or are we just existing?

Take a look at the jobs you have been applying for. What kinds of jobs are they? Would they be considered *entry-level*? If so, then the recruiter is probably getting a ton of resumes. Even if you fit the job description to a "T," maybe your work history is spotty or your reasons for leaving less than appealing. No matter who you are or what your job experience is, there will always be competition.

Understand this simple thought: Your resume is sometimes the ONLY thing you have to get you to that next step. It is either what gets your foot in the door or what slams it shut in your face. Your first job, to the best of your ability, is to make sure that your resume accurately reflects who you are and what you have done.

One of the common mistakes I see on resumes is T.M.I. – Too Much Information! I am aware that you want the prospective employer to know everything (good) about you; all your skills, talents and experience. HOWEVER, remember this: Most of the time, we recruiters and hiring managers do not have the TIME to spend reading about everything you have done in your life! We want to be able to see exactly what we are looking for as clearly and concisely as possible. Do not stand out in a *bad* way by overloading us with information that may not apply to the position you are seeking.

My advice? Do not spend a bunch of time listing every skill you have. Get right to the point. List your most recent work history first and go backward chronologically. This is especially true for those entry-level jobs where there might be a lot of competition. I have seen as many as 500 applications a week for some jobs! I DO NOT HAVE TIME to scrutinize EVERY little detail of your work life. Really.

Start to think like a recruiter. What would YOU want to see on a resume if you were looking to hire someone? Now, that does not mean you have to be boring. No. But it does mean that you have to get to the point first AND make an impression.

Things that irk me (my pet peeves) on a resume are MISSPELLED words! Argh!! Do not just settle for the spell-check function. Here is a thought, how about actually READING your own resume? Better yet, why not also have a friend, or two, actually read your resume?

I will tell you why. There is such a word as "costumer." This is a person who creates and assembles costumes. It is NOT, however, the same as a "customer," as in one who buys goods or services from a store. Get it? Spell-check would not catch that because they are both words. But "costumer" is probably not the word you meant to have in your resume when applying for a Customer Service position, right?

Another example: "Manger." This is an eating trough for animals, NOT a "manager" who directs a business or enterprise. Again, please read your resumes!

"Filling." What are you filling? Or did you mean "filing?" Were you "preformed" or have you "performed?" You get the idea.

Have a resume-reading party. Get a couple of friends together at a coffee shop and pass your resumes around the table. At the end, ask each of your friends to talk about themselves and what their work history is. How effective was your resume in reflecting your skills, abilities and experience?

One last little tidbit: If you cannot even spell your own name correctly on an online application, chances are good that the recruiter will try to make a proverbial "swish" with your application as it is, what? That's right, shot into the round FILE that is now FILLED with all the other misspelled resumes!

Here are some other things to keep in mind: Does your resume make sense? Does it flow well? How many pages is it? Is it visually appealing? Are there certain words in **BOLD** that are appropriate to catch the reader's eye? •Bullet points? <u>Underlined?</u> *Italicized*? While you are all sitting around drinking coffee at your resume-reading party, ask your friends to look at these aspects as well.

Another important thing: Please put the dates of employment on your resume. Please? And not just "2010-2011."

Let's think about that. It could have been 12/10 to 01/11 (2 months) =OR= it could have been 01/10 to 12/11, right? Two years! Don't you want the person reading your resume to know that you worked there for more than two months? Guess what? A good recruiter gets annoyed with stuff like that, and we may even tend to think that a person is avoiding the truth about their work history if they are not more clear.

S E C T I O N 3: RESUME-WRITING

* * * * * * *

"You call THIS a resume?"

Here are excerpts from two resumes that made me pull my hair out. I simply copied and pasted them straight from the online application, removing all identifying factors to protect them from public humiliation. Perhaps they might even read this book and learn something.

First *bad resume* example:

Resume
I am forwarding my resume for this open position. Thank you for your consideration. Briefly to explain the lapse in work dates years ago I was injured on the job and had a back surgery. I went into a retraining program which do to economical struggles failed to finish my training and has closed down a large portion of the company. The school shut down in 2008. I have been left with out proper training to get employment in the dental lab area so I am looking elsewhere.

– First Name, Last Name

--- Job Objective ---
To eventually obtain a full-time position that will allow me to use my public relations and customer service skills in a positive work environment.

-------------- Professional Achievements-------------
Denture Masters Laboratory/XXXX Institute Of Dental Technology.
Administrative Advisor/ Laboratory Manager, 2006-2008. Wage $XX.XX
hr. w/car and gasoline. Paid cellular phone account /phone. * Promoted
from Dental Laboratory Technician to Administrative Advisor after
completing one year of dental technician training at the XXXX Institute
Of Dental Technology.
Direct liaison between doctor/CEO of Denture Masters Laboratory, XXXX
Institute of Dental Technology and students, lab technicians to direct
and motivate in order to achieve company goals. Researching and
applying for qualifying grants to advance the XIDT...

Honestly? Is this a resume you even WANT to read? There was so
much information and so little attractiveness about it, I became
disinterested the moment I saw it. I spared you by not sharing the
rest of the 200+ words with no line breaks.

Second *bad resume* example:

Objective

College bound student seeking Fulltime Employment or related focused program of studies.

Experience

Customer Service Sales Reprehensive –MACY'S ,XXXX, XX   May 2007-Presnet

- Product merchandising ,product endorsement,
- Controlling Inventory, Meeting sales explications
- Cashiering, stocking merchandise, keeping up with product knowledge

Sales Associate- The XXX Store , XXXX, XX   September 2007

- Packaging, selling , customer service
- Marketing XXX sales , cashiering , phone orders
- On call staffing , customer assistant on packaging

Education

XXX University   June 2007-Present

Psychology programs to expanding my knowledge and skills for a health field or related jobs.

Marketing Retail June 2008-Present

Marketing management and product placement courses for other focus programs of study.

Skills

Studying psychology gives you skills in planning, conducting and evaluating experiments and researching and interpreting scientific literature. I am very fluent in analytical and problem-solving, computing and statistics - using spreadsheets, databases and presentation packages, data interpretation and management. Numeric organization - acquired through coping with your workload of lectures, practical, study, part-time work, social activities. The ability to identify, select, organize and communicate information, team working - learned through your laboratory work, or perhaps through sport, joining a society or volunteering.

Okay. What exactly is a "Customer Service Reprehensive" anyway? And how about a "presnet?" Were they packaging and selling customer service? This person then lists studying psychology and how it "gives you skills in planning... and interpreting scientific literature." Huh?

S E C T I O N 3: RESUME-WRITING

* * * * * * *

Putting it Together
(Your Resume)

There are a lot of different philosophies out there about how a resume should look. Different experts have different opinions about what is right and wrong in resume-writing. So, to cut through all of that, I am just going to tell what I like and do not like to see on a resume.

Objective Statements: If I could do away with these, I would. I rarely ever read them! Why? Because they all say the same thing: "I want a job." Duh! Let's get creative here, folks. You are not a "cookie-cutter" person. You have unique and wonderful qualities that make you special. Why get stuck in a format or cookie-cutter template? You are not a template, are you? Then make sure your resume shows that!

Remember that this resume is the ONLY thing you have to get you through to that next step! Its ONLY purpose is to get you in front of someone (either over the phone or in person). So – it has got to POP! It has to STAND OUT (in a good way).

I am always more interested and impressed when I see "Mission Statement" or "Personal Statement" at the top of a resume. My own personal resume has these words across the top, just under my name and phone number: "Committed, Effective, Direct, Leader, Crazy."

Yes, "Crazy." Why? Because I want to stand out. I want people to stop and re-read that word. I want them to ask themselves, "What kind of person would have the guts (or stupidity?) to put something like that on their resume?" Exaaactly. What kind of person would do that? A risk-taker? Someone who thinks outside the box? A person with a sense of humor, perhaps? At any rate, they remembered me and called me – if for no other reason than to find out who would do something like that. In fact, there were many calls, and the first thing I was asked was, "So… 'crazy,' huh?"

Now, the flip side to that is that it may turn someone off or disinterest them. Okay. That was the risk I took with a word like that. But then, do I want to work for a person or a company who doesn't get it? Probably not for me.

Remember: It is all in the presentation!

You can list your occupation as a "Customer Service Rep" =OR= you can tell me you did this: "I had friendly conversations with customers, practiced critical thinking and emphasized great teamwork." If you were looking at 500 resumes a week, which one would stand out in your mind?

Another piece of advice: There are many jobs in which the basic duties are understood, such as a receptionist. You answer the phone, do some filing and various office tasks. Instead of listing these commonalities, why not tell us what you did to save the company money, increase productivity or create a new process that is still being used in the company today? What made you stand out from the rest?

The "Shotgun vs. Sniper" approach to job seeking: When you shoot a shotgun, the bullets spray everywhere. This is the approach we recruiters see as "desperate." Someone is just applying for anything and everything without the benefit of really doing their homework (reading the job description and requirements of the job, or researching the company on-line). If you are applying for the Administrative Assistant AND the CFO of a corporation, what does that tell me? You are taking the shotgun approach!

Think of it this way: As a corporate recruiter, I can see EVERY job you applied for at my company. Every single one. So, if you want me to take you seriously, please be aware of what you are applying for and make sure that it makes sense!

Snipers' rifles are precise and to the point. If all the jobs you have applied for are within the same skill set, that tells us that you are really paying attention, doing your research and that you have given careful consideration to the positions for which you are spending your time applying. It will also reveal (by your resume) whether or not you have a good sense of your capabilities and who you are.

Your resume should be an accurate depiction of YOU! It needs to be well thought out, balanced (not TMI) and to the point. The point in creating your resume is to just start. That first resume may not end up being the one you stick with, but you have to start somewhere. Change what you need to, have your friends critique it, observe what gets talked about when someone does call you for an interview, and think of it as a "work in progress." Just like you are.

Resume templates are a good way to get started. But use them as a reference only. You can gain ideas about what to do and what not to do. Also be aware that it can often be difficult to make changes when using a template. So, again, take in all the information you can about them and what they look like, but apply yourself to creating one that accurately tells me who you are and what you have done.

Sometimes it is hard to know what a company description is and the pay grade or level they are willing to pay. Again, do your homework. Check out: salary.com and other sites designed to give you an idea of the median salary of your occupation that is based on several factors.

The "salary expectation" question is a hard one. Most people struggle with how to answer that. From a recruiter's standpoint, it is critical that you do not play games. Come up with a comfortable answer ahead of time. If you can state what your minimum salary requirements are, along with a comfortable "range" you are willing to accept, it gives us a better idea of what we are working with.

The reason for this is because many times there is a budgeted salary amount or range for the position you are seeking. Some companies pay higher, some lower. Consider all the factors when answering this question. What are the benefits? How stable is this company? Are you willing to take a more entry-level position to get your foot in the door?

If so, do not talk about wanting to move up in the company right away, because there might be the expectation that you stay in that position for at least a year before seeking a promotion or different position. Remember that it takes a lot of money to hire, train and develop new employees. Do not give your prospective employer the idea that you are just interested in his/her position just to get somewhere else within the company.

Bottom line is to be prepared with an answer that ANSWERS the question!

SECTION 4: THE PHONE INTERVIEW

* * * * * * *

Please understand this: Once you hit that "Apply Now" button, you are "On." In other words, your resume and phone number are now out there. Every interaction you have going forward could be a potential employer! Be prepared for that phone call from a recruiter at any time after that.

Make sure your ring back tone and outgoing message is appropriate. "Shorty get your thang on," is NOT appropriate for a potential employer to hear!

Please be sure that if someone else is answering your phone (or you have given another person's phone number as a call back) that you let them know you are looking for work and to please be POLITE when answering calls because it could be a potential employer. You would not believe the number of "Yea? Who's this?!" greetings I get. People are sometimes very rude. Do not assume it is a bill collector or telemarketer. BE POLITE! Answer your phone professionally.

The funniest thing to me is when I am making a call and the person answers and sounds just plain, old "blah." But as soon as I introduce myself, I hear, "OH, Hiiiii!!!" Big smiley face! Absolutely hilarious! Just be upbeat with every call. And hey, if it IS a bill collector, being polite to them is a good thing anyway.

One misconception is this: You do not have to try to talk to that person right then and there if you are preoccupied or busy. It really is OKAY to tell the person calling that now is not an ideal time for you. And do not even think about answering the phone if you are on the toilet, okay? We can hear the flush!

But seriously, if you are about to go in to your doctor's office or your kids are screaming in the background, these are those "stand out in a bad way" situations. I would really prefer to talk to you when you are uninterrupted and in a quiet space. It is better for BOTH of us.

Listen, we understand that we often call at times when you are busy living your life. But do you remember hitting that "Apply Now" button? Politely tell the recruiter, "I'd really like to give you my full attention. Now is not the ideal time for me to do that. May I take your number and call you back? What is the best time to reach you?"

This is perfectly fine with us. In fact, we would PREFER you do this rather than trying to conduct a phone interview when you are distracted. Also, when the phone rings, turn the TV off or go into another room! You never know who is calling, and right off the bat it sends a message (not necessarily a good one) when you answer your phone.

What am I listening for when I call you? Lots of things. Experienced recruiters know we can learn a lot about a person, not only by the way they answer the phone, but by the things they say.

It may seem redundant to you when we ask about your current and past jobs; going over skills and duties. We do this because we are listening for what comes out of your mouth regarding priorities and what you deemed the most important aspects of your past jobs. We want to hear how you communicate and how motivated you are to work for our company.

If I ask you to tell me what your duties and responsibilities were at your last job and the first thing you tell me is that you "had to deal with angry customers," what do you think I get from that? You had to "deal with," rather than "work with." Is there a possible underlying negative aspect to this? If the first thing you talk about is angry customers and not something positive, is that possibly an indication of your personal outlook on life? These are all subjective, yes, but keep in mind that a good recruiter is also very adept at reading people.

I am going to ask you why you left your previous employers. Then I will ask you HOW you left your previous employers. Did you give two-weeks notice and stay the entire time? I am listening carefully to the reasons you give for moving on.

In these days, many, many people are losing their jobs due to down-sizing, lay-offs, early retirements, etc. These are valid reasons and not necessarily your fault. But if your explanation is that you quit your last job, I will ask you for more information. What do you mean by "quit?" Instead, say you had another opportunity and gave notice. The word "quit" gives a negative connotation. It makes us think you just threw your keys on the floor and walked out the door in a huff. "I QUIT!!!"

Some catch-phrases to be aware of (and I am personally sick of hearing): "I'm a people-person," or "I learn quickly." If you truly wish to convey that you enjoy interacting with people because it gives you a sense of accomplishment by helping make their day better, then say THAT. TELL me about a time you had to learn something, then go into more specifics about how quickly you picked it up. Remember: You are not cookie-cutter people, so really work on not making your answers cookie-cutter either.

This is something that annoys me: Someone applies for a job, then GOES ON VACATION! What happens when you are on vacation? Do you answer your phone the same way (if at all), than you would if you were back home? Probably not. What if you go camping in the Siskiyou Mountains and your cell phone cannot get reception?

Now, I understand that life happens. Sometimes we are called away for family emergencies or a trip to Paris. If that happens, make sure you are either answering your phone or changing the outgoing message to reflect that you are out of the country or had to attend to a family emergency. Otherwise, the recruiter may call you only once, and if he or she has not heard back from you after a few days, will give up. Remember, for every position open, there are anywhere from 10 to 100 people (or more) vying for that position who DO answer their phones and return calls immediately.

Again, Too Much Information (TMI): Listen, I know you might be nervous when you talk to me, but please, please think about what you say to me over the phone. Do not go into why you had to leave your last job with too much personal information. For instance, your son is sick with a rare disease and needed to be bathed and fed and you had to learn how to give him his medications and change his bedding every four hours and THAT is why you left your last job. Whew! You just overloaded me with TMI.

I do not need to know all the gory details. While I may care on a personal level, this is a professional interaction. This leaves the door open to too many possibilities. WHY you are telling me all of this? Are you trying to elicit sympathy from me or impress me with your medical knowledge? Either way, it is probably not appropriate information for me to know. Period.

The same thing goes for illnesses and injuries you have had. It is better for you if you KISS (Keep It Simple Sweetie).

When leaving a message to return my call – please do not tell me why you did not answer the phone the first time, especially when it is too personal. I have actually had people tell me they were in the shower, on the toilet or having sex (so not kidding on that one). I – do - not – need – to – know – these – things!!

S E C T I O N 4: THE PHONE INTERVIEW

* * * * * *

Making Excuses
(over the phone or in person)

This probably won't be a very popular subject with some of you, but I have to "go there" any way.

Sometimes people give more reasons why they CANNOT do something, and spend more time complaining and making excuses for their inaction, than telling me why they are the best person for the job. It is a cop-out. No matter your situation, there is always something POSITIVE you can do with your life, including finding employment, that will not only sustain you but enhance your life; so stick to the "Can Do" attitude, not excuses for why you "Can't Do."

There is no doubt that people have challenges! One of the groups I volunteer with is a prison here in Portland. Every other month I present to a group of men who will soon be released back into their communities. Now, THESE guys have challenges!

They are re-entering a society in which the economy is still struggling (at the time of this writing). They also have the stigma of being formally incarcerated. Many times they are also people of color. Keep in mind that the published unemployment rate does not accurately reflect the unemployment rate for people of color, veterans, people with legal histories or those who are differently-abled.

S E C T I O N 4: THE PHONE INTERVIEW

* * * * * * *

A Story:
The Bridge and Mr. Perseverance

I met "Mr. Perseverance" (Mr. P) in early 1998 in Palo Alto, CA. I had just begun working at Manpower Temporary Services as a Staffing Specialist. My office was a mile from Stanford University, right on University Avenue. My job was to interview and place people on temporary assignments within companies with whom we contracted.

No one in Palo Alto needed work. This was one of the most affluent communities in the Bay area. Almost all of the temporary workers who were employed by us were from East Palo Alto (EPA), just across Hwy 101. Cross that highway and you enter another world. Residents in EPA typically lived a low-income, high-crime life of struggle and disappointment. In fact, when I first moved to that area (the previous month), I was told to avoid EPA at all costs.

I met Mr. P through a phone call I placed in order to take him off an assignment that had ended. He was upset about it, but being new, I told him there was nothing I could do about it and quickly hung up the phone. The next day, while working at my desk, I heard a voice behind me asking if I were "Shauna." When I turned around, I saw a very large, Black man standing there. It surprised me because his voice was so soft. It was Mr. P.

Although intimidated by his size, there was something immediately noticeable in his composure. He approached me with hesitancy and respect. He did not immediately launch into a tirade about needing work. Instead, he asked if he could talk with me. I welcomed him to sit down.

What I learned about him was that he had, in fact, just gotten out of San Quentin prison and did not have a permanent residence. When I asked if he had a resume, he replied, "What's a resume?"

There was an innocence and naïveté about him that was endearing, so I opened a new Word document and began asking him about his work history. We created a resume as we spoke.

After we finished, I made several copies and began to send him on his way, then stopped, looked him directly in the eyes and asked, "Is this the kind of life you want to live?" He emphatically told me that it was not, but he just needed someone to give him a chance.

So I looked up our open jobs and found an assignment I thought he could do. He was to report to work the next morning at 6:30 a.m. As I handed him the information, I looked him directly in the eyes again and said, "Here's a job assignment for you. You have to be there at 6:30 in the morning. CAN YOU DO THAT?"

He answered, "Yes! I will be there."

I said, "Good, because you only get one chance with me. If you blow this, that's it. Got it?"

He replied, "Okay," and went on his way.

The next morning, I called the employer and found out that Mr. P had, in fact, shown up on time and had even been a little early. He was already doing a good job and the employer was happy with him. Throughout the next week or so, I checked on Mr. P several times and found that he had consistently been on time and the employer really liked him.

When he came in to get his first paycheck, he sat down at my desk and I congratulated him. I told him I was proud of him and thanked him for his efforts. That's when I found out that he had been getting up at 4:00 a.m. and walking across the Dumbarton Bridge, in order to get to this employer on time every day.

The Dumbarton Bridge is nearly two miles long with a very narrow shoulder, yet, this big guy was walking it twice a day, every day, to keep his commitment. This so impressed me that when his assignment ended, I made sure to keep him working.

Mr. Perseverance always came by on payday and sometimes during the week just to sit and visit with me. He would ask how my day was going and always seemed genuinely interested. He continued to get high marks from the employers he worked with, so became my "go-to" guy when any of us needed someone reliable on an assignment. After a couple of months, we had become friends.

He never let me down and when I left California, he had a temp-to-hire job at a manufacturing company that was paying a very good wage.

So when someone tells me that they just "can't work," I like to share this story as an example of what one person did.

SECTION 5: THE IN-PERSON INTERVIEW

* * * * * * *

What is the number one documented fear people have? Yep, you guessed it – public speaking. And the in-person interview might as well be public speaking, because you are definitely "on stage" in front of a very important audience – your potential new boss!

So let's explore some possible reasons people are so afraid of this wonderful opportunity to be seen and heard.

1. Low self-confidence: My hair is too bushy (or flat); my teeth aren't straight (or white); I have a lisp (or a stutter); they'll see all of my imperfections, or I haven't worked in so long, they won't give me the job because of it.

2. No experience or a bad experience: I've never gone to an interview before; I had a bad experience that didn't end well and it's stuck in my mind.

3. Made up fear: This is something you have manufactured in your own mind and it is manifesting itself in your body (sweaty palms, nervous twitch, racing heart). You believe it is real and therefore it becomes a self-fulfilling prophecy. It IS real.

Not many of us have a realistic view of ourselves. We always want what we do not have because we perceive this to be the cure for our unhappiness – money, good looks, a model figure, a winning smile. When we carry this baggage into our interviews with us, it comes through the door before WE do!

Now, I am not saying that you have to go to psychotherapy before an interview, but I am saying that you do need to have an honest conversation with yourself. Focus on the good things about you. SEE them! Give yourself a little pep talk. After all, if you do not at least begin to believe in yourself, how do you expect others to?

Fake it 'til you MAKE it! In other words, pretend to have a good (but not overly boastful) self-esteem. Smile! Feign self-confidence. BE that person you want to be. Now walk into that room and nail that interview!!

Maybe you had a bad experience in an interview before? So what? Are you going to hang on to that for the rest of your life? Cut it loose! That was then; this is now. It is what it is – a PAST experience. Now you know better (hopefully) and when you know better, you DO better.

S E C T I O N 5: THE IN-PERSON INTERVIEW

* * * * * * *

A Story:

Nervous is Good

When I was in third grade, I got a part in the school play. I was the Narrator. This meant that I had a speaking part in every, single act of that play. Mind you, I was nine years old.

I remember walking down the dark, empty hall of my elementary school on my way to the gym where everyone was preparing for the play – the band was warming up and actors were rehearsing lines as the stage hands prepared for the first scene. It was evening. I do not actually remember why I was alone, only that I could hardly breathe from fear of what I was about to do.

For weeks I rehearsed my lines over and over with my mother, who had won many awards for interpretive reading and oratory in high school. I practiced commanding my little-girl-voice to "boom" out to the audience without it sounding like I was trying too hard.

As I was deep in thought and trying to find a reason why I shouldn't just run away or hide in the broom closet, one of the third-grade teachers suddenly appeared next to me in the hall. She was the piano player for the play.

Mrs. Larsen was a scary woman. Not only was she super tall, she also had a hump in her back and didn't exactly have the face of a Madonna. I was startled and must have made a sound depicting that.

"On your way to the play? You're the Narrator, aren't you?" She had never spoken to me before and her voice was a little deeper than I thought it should be.

Wide-eyed, I looked (waaay up) at her and nodded.

"Are you nervous?" she asked.

I tried to speak, but sawdust came out. "Waahaak ah hiiem…"

She chuckled. "Well, that's GOOD!!" she said.

Como, say WHAT?!

Mrs. Larsen went on to tell me that in her very first piano recital, she had not been nervous at all. She flubbed the notes in the middle of her performance and afterward, mortified and embarrassed, could barely hear her mother telling her that it was a good thing to be a little nervous. She explained that being nervous made you more prepared because the adrenalin in your body kept you ready for a "fight." In other words, being too relaxed would not give you the edge needed to perform at your best. Nerves (adrenalin) make you focused and aware of the task at hand.

She put her hand on my shoulder. "It's a good thing to be comfortable with your nervousness, Honey. Just remember that and you'll always do well."

As she passed me with those spider legs and awkward stride, her words echoed in my mind. I was suddenly standing a little taller.

"Well, I've got nothing to lose. Why not try it?" I made myself relax into that nervousness and used it to get through that night and the following night at our final performance. Mrs. Larsen's words have stayed with me throughout my life.

S E C T I O N 5: THE IN-PERSON INTERVIEW

* * * * * * *

Be Prepared

One way to be comfortable with your nervousness is to prepare for the interview.

Keep several copies of your resume in a folder near the door to remind you when you leave. If you have awards, certificates of achievement, great sales records or letters of recommendation, bring those as well.

Know the location by checking Google Maps, Mapquest or GPS, then GO to that location the day before. Check it out. What are the parking options and street signs like? Is there a lot of traffic? If you ride a bus, find the schedule for drop-off at that location and take the earlier bus. That way, when life happens, you will not be late (hopefully).

Make sure you know the room, suite or floor number where you are meeting the interviewer and, by all means, know that person's NAME and phone number or extension. That way, if you are running late on the day of your interview, you can call and leave a message. Even though that situation is not ideal, we do appreciate hearing from you, and most of the time we will understand. Give an explanation – the bus was late or there was an accident, etc. – not that you woke up late!

Always dress UP for an interview. Period. Even an interview for a warehouse or heavy-labor job warrants your Sunday best. If you think that you might get hired on the spot, bring your work clothes with you. You are selling yourself, so you need to present yourself in the best manner possible. It is important to give a good first impression because that is what usually remains in the interviewer's mind after you leave.

Men: Slacks and button-down shirts with a tie is appropriate attire unless you are interviewing for a business position. You will need to wear a well-fitted suit for this. Please be well-groomed. That means, brush your teeth and hair! Wash your face. Take a shower, put on some cologne – but not too much! I cannot tell you how many times I have been distracted by some food item stuck in someone's un-brushed teeth, uncombed hair or overwhelming cologne usage. Remember: Stand out in a *good* way!

Women: Nice dress slacks and a blouse would be fine – suit or dress optional depending on the position you are interviewing for. Dress in something loose or comfortable for you. Do not try to impress us with a low-cut top. We do not want to see your boobies! While some may be intrigued by what they see, the vast majority interviewing you will be unimpressed with your obvious attempt to grab attention. It sends the wrong message and no one will be concentrating on what you have to SAY. Same thing goes for extremely high heels. I remember an interview in which a woman came in wearing five-inch stilettos. I just kept thinking, "How in the world is she walking in those?!" rather than who she was as a person.

Men AND Women: You want to stand out in a GOOD way, remember? Typical business attire can be boring (black, grey or dark blue). So if you want to stand out, wear a color that "pops," such as a brightly-colored scarf, blouse or tie.

Body piercings and Tats: Being an individual is a good thing. Expressing yourself is also a good thing. Appropriate for an interview? Maybe not. Consider your audience. If you are interviewing for a professional position in a conservative office setting, then find a way to cover those tats up and take out that nose, tongue or eyebrow ring. If you feel comfortable, ask the interviewer about the company dress code. What is acceptable and what is not? If they look at you funny, be honest and up-front about it. Tell them about the tattoos or nose ring. They will appreciate your honesty.

DO NOT SMOKE right before your interview! I realize many smokers feel it "calms the nerves," but please do not do it. We smell it. Trust me. Even if we smoke as well, it leaves a bad impression.

Nervous habits during the interview (fidgeting, toe-tapping and yes, hair poking): If you know that you have a problem with this, find an alternative. Practice sitting with your hands in your lap. Take a pen into the interview and hold on to it for dear life, if you must. Grab the bottom of the chair with your hands and pull up.

If you are a knee-shaker, plant your feet solidly on the floor and place your hands on your knees. This will subconsciously help you because you can literally hold them down with your hands. If that knee does start shaking, your whole body will move and that should "shake" you out of it (literally).

My wonderful and unique daughter has a strange habit. She has very long hair and will take a few strands from the back of her neck, pull them down to the tips of her fingers and then proceed to poke the ends of her hair on her lips or chin. She says this calms her and helps her to focus. I say she's really weird. But then, in our family "weird" is a good thing. My point is, if you know you have a propensity to do something like this, find a way NOT to do it during the interview. It will distract us at the very least and may confuse and annoy us at the most. In the end, *we are not paying attention to what you are SAYING!!*

Practice looking people in the eye. Do not stare above our heads, at our mouths or out the window behind us. Look your interviewer in the eyes! If you do not, this gives the impression that you are either hiding something or you are just a little strange. But we do not need to have a staring contest either, so learn to look away at appropriate times.

SMILE! This is THE best thing you can wear to an interview. Seriously. Many times when people are nervous or concentrating they can appear to be angry or distracted. If you practice smiling, it will come easier and more natural – even during an interview. Remember that the person interviewing you might be a little nervous too, so give a smile that says that you are at ease (even if you are not). This helps us to relax as well!

One further point: Interviewers (hiring managers, HR people and recruiters), may not be as experienced in interviewing as you think. So here is a little clue: We are human too. I know that may sound silly, but sometimes people forget that.

Remember, you could very well be the first applicant your interviewer has ever interviewed. Maybe he or she is just a little rusty with the process. Being unprepared with the right questions, not keeping the interview flowing well, or being distracted about the next meeting can all contribute to an uncomfortable interview. And that would not be your fault!

But you must be prepared for anything. Keep focused and KEEP THE PERSON INTERESTED IN YOU. This could even work in your favor by demonstrating your patience, concentration and leadership skills. And that will make you stand out in a *good* way.

Hopefully when you realize that the person on the other side of that desk is just like you, it will help to alleviate some of your fears. Pretend you just met at a party or networking event. Be genuinely interested in your interviewer and the company. You can ask questions too. What are our interests, skills and experience? Remember the "informational interview" I talked about earlier? Same concept. Just remember that you have to balance the interview. Do not start barking out questions until we have finished with ours.

Practice. Practice. Practice!!

Interviewing well is an art – like learning how to play an instrument or improving your batting average. If you do not practice, you can never achieve perfection. Try conducting some "mock" interviews with your friends who are serious about helping you in your job search. Do not do this with your buddy who snickers or asks you trick or ridiculous questions!

The more you do this, the more comfortable you are with the process, the better you present yourself! This is especially true if your mock interviewer gives you helpful feedback. Many times we are so focused on what we say, that we are not aware of what our bodies are doing or how our facial expressions are being perceived. When someone tells you (or shows you by video-taping), you will be one step ahead of every one else being interviewed.

* * * * * * *

Behavioral Interviewing

These questions require more than one- or two-word answers. Most companies today use this style. The point is for you to draw from your past experiences and *tell us a story* about how you handled different issues. Do not answer with, "Well, what I *would* do...."

Rather try, "I was working at ABC company as the office assistant when one of my co-workers...."

We ask these kinds of questions because we know that the way you handled something in the past is a good indicator of how you will handle similar situations in our company.

There will be some tough questions. So before you walk into that interview, have a few examples prepared so that you can pull them out of your back pocket (not literally), if necessary. Write them down and study them before the interview so they are fresh in your mind. The reason I say this is because when most of us are nervous, we can barely remember what our names are, let alone give good examples to the following questions:

1. When were you a *star*? For example, how did you save the company money, prevent fraud, create a new process or help diffuse a situation with a customer or co-worker?

2. Is there a time when you did not perform well, or were you ever terminated? What did you do, and more importantly, what did you learn so you will not make that same mistake again?

3. Can you remember a time when you were asked to do something you believed was wrong? What was the situation and how did you handle it?

4. Can you talk about a time when you went above and beyond the call of duty for a customer?

5. What are your strengths AND areas for improvement? Be honest with yourself about this. But be prepared to talk about it so that you come across confident, but not cocky. Regarding areas of improvement, do not answer with, "I work too hard," or "I don't delegate my work. I just want to do it ALL!" Be truthful, but always be able to describe how you are working to improve this now.

For additional ideas on interview questions, the internet is a wonderful and useful tool.

S E C T I O N 5: THE IN-PERSON INTERVIEW

* * * * * * *

A Story:
Proud Mama

My hair-poking daughter is a great example of being prepared for an interview. When she was just 15 years old, she decided she wanted to get a job during the summer. She applied for and got an interview at a major retail store.

To prepare, she looked the company up on the internet and memorized some key points about the company – when it was established and something she admired about them. She also looked up typical interview questions and wrote down her answers to some of them.

On the day of the interview she wore a skirt and button down blouse with her hair pulled up, conservative make-up and most importantly, a smile. I drove her to the interview 15 minutes early so she could be directed to the correct floor where her interviewer was waiting for her.

She got out of the car, turned and smiled at me. I said, "Good luck, honey!" She walked into the store and I drove home, extremely proud of her. She got the job!

The following Monday at the new employee orientation, she filled out the forms, including the I-9 (for employment eligibility). It was then discovered that she was actually under age for that particular job and they were unable to continue her employment. She was devastated.

However, two weeks later, I was at a training seminar for The United Way campaign coordinators. The woman in front of me was signing in. I happened to see her name as she signed it and realized she was the person who had interviewed my daughter. I knew this because she had a very unique name. I introduced myself. When I told her who my daughter was, her entire face lit up and she said, "Oh, my gosh! Please tell your daughter to call me the minute she turns 16! We were so impressed with her that we just assumed she was older. She has a job with us any time!"

SECTION 5: THE IN-PERSON INTERVIEW

* * * * * * *

At the End of the Interview

Prospective employers will usually ask if you have any questions. You should be prepared for this.

Please do not make the mistake of asking about pay and benefits at this time. This is way too assumptive and could turn them off or give them the impression that this is all you care about, instead of the job itself. Remember about listening for clues about a person's true intent in the phone interview? Same thing applies here.

People tend to enjoy talking about themselves or their career. Ask something specific of the interviewer like, "What do YOU enjoy about working here?" or, "What are some challenges you have faced working here?" or, "Do the company goals match your own personal goals and if so, how?"

It is up to you what to ask, but be sure to have at least a couple of questions in mind.

It IS okay to ask about the hiring process. I would not ask, "How did I do?" however. A better question might be, "I've really enjoyed my time with you and look forward to the next step. Can you tell me what that is?"

Remember a simple truth: Saying, "Thank you," goes a long way. In person is always best, so remember to look your interviewer straight in the eye, smile, give a strong handshake and say, "Thank you." It gives a great last impression.

SECTION 6: THE FOLLOW-UP

* * * * * * *

Now what? You have followed this advice. You have planned, prepared, performed and now you must do the hardest part – persevere. This means that you do not let *defeat* defeat you. Keep trying. Keep perfecting your plan. Do not give up!

Keep yourself fresh in your interviewer's mind by sending a follow-up email or card. Keep it professional but personable. Refer to something said in the interview if appropriate.

Even if the company chooses another candidate, you might be their second choice. Maintaining a good connection can also yield results. Never burn bridges. You may be disappointed that you did not get that particular job, but you never know what may be available next. That person may be able to help you or advocate for you to get the next job.

If you have built a rapport with the recruiter or hiring manager, sometimes you can ask for advice on your interviewing skills. Perhaps it was something you did, or did not, say that made the difference between you and the person who got the job. The key to this is making the recruiter feel comfortable (and not threatened), by telling you the whole truth.

As a recruiter, I believe people want this truth. Not everyone is prepared for it, however. What I usually do when asked, is to ask a question in return: "Do you want me to be honest with you?"

What I mean by this is, "I will be honest because I want to help and encourage you for your next interview, however, the truth might sting a little."

SECTION 6: THE FOLLOW-UP

* * * * * * *

A Story:
Mr. Clean on Steroids

I was in the prison talking to a group of about 20 inmates. It was toward the end of my presentation, so I had gotten to know them a little better. One man in particular seemed really interested in what I had to say. At one point in the presentation, when I was talking about email addresses and what was appropriate for them, he raised his hand.

"What's email?" He asked.

Whoa! There was silence. Thankfully, the other guys did not embarrass him, but there was an obvious hush in the room because this guy had clearly been down for quite some time. I hardly skipped a beat and told him what it was.

Later, we were talking about first impressions when showing up for an interview. He raised his hand again and asked me what I thought people would think about him. I looked at him. This guy was very tall, broad shouldered, bald and had a very intimidating look to him. I will be frank. He looked like Mr. Clean on steroids. He was pretty scary-looking.

I asked him, "Do you want me to be completely honest with you?"

He nodded, "Yes."

I replied, "You're kind of scary-looking. But I've noticed that when you smile, your whole face and demeanor changes. To change people's perception of you, I would try to smile more. I don't mean going around 'cheesing' at everyone all the time, but be more aware of how you might come across and smile more."

There was a kind of electricity in the air while we all took a collective breath and waited.

He sat down, looked at me and said, "I know. I do look kinda mean. I just haven't had a lot to smile about these past 30 years in prison. That's good advice though. Thank you."

At the end, he waited while everyone was filing out of the room. I greeted him with a smile and a handshake.

"Hey, I hope you weren't offended by what I said."

He *smiled*. "No. I needed to hear it. No one ever says things like that to me. It's probably because I do intimidate people by the way I look."

Then he chuckled and thanked me for being honest with him. Whew!!

CONCLUSION

* * * * * * *

In a recent conversation, my youngest sister, who is a practicing psychologist, asked me what my purpose in life is. That is not an easy question to answer. I thought back to my early days of recruiting and remembered one man in particular. I cannot remember his name, only that he was someone I had given that "tough love" to in my very real approach with people.

He stood in front of me and looked me directly in the eyes. He said, "Shauna, you made all the difference in the world to me. If it hadn't been for you being so real and honest with me and giving me the chance you did, I don't know where I'd be today. Thank you."

It was one of the most powerful encounters I've ever had. I knew in that moment that I had changed his life in a very positive way. I had made a difference.

That was the moment I became hooked.

Now, when I speak to groups or individuals and see that light bulb turn on in their eyes and hear, "I've never thought about it that way before!" THAT is my reward. It is what keeps me doing what I do.

It is my hope and prayer that this book has done the same for you.

–END –

THANK YOU.

People often thank God first, and I am no exception. Truthfully He *is* the reason for my joy and I give Him all the glory and honor just for being God – all by Himself! I would not be where I am today if it had not been for His light in my life.

Ramey, my sister, my friend, my war-buddy. There are not words to express my gratitude. Your talent and work come from a place within you that makes you unforgettable and unique. I love you.

Janell Denk. What a heart for God you have! Thank you for your wonderful photos and warm spirit.

Gretchen: You will always be my best friend. You know too much! 'Nuff said . . . .

Abdul and Andy: You humble me. Thank you.

Mom: You are a beautiful woman. Thank you for your intelligence and PATIENCE with me over the years. Thank you for always loving me. I love you back.

My Mariah and Chante: My reason for existing. Mommy is SO proud of both of you. You are my heart. Go after your dreams and never let others define you. Stand strong, my girls. Be you. Amazing, beautiful YOU!

Lastly, my husband Charles: You started all of this! Not only do I continue to do this work because of you, but this book was inspired from how you changed my life . You set me on the path I am on today and I have been truly blessed having you in my life. Thank you for loving me and helping to heal me. I love and adore you.

www.ingramcontent.com/pod-product-compliance
Lightning Source LLC
Chambersburg PA
CBHW051220170526
45166CB00005B/1971